Non-fic Voyage 4

Series Advisers
Shirley Bickler and Raewyn Hickey

Contents

OXFORD
UNIVERSITY PRESS

Paul McCartney

Paul McCartney is the most successful composer in pop music history. He has had 30 top ten singles in the USA and Britain – even though he can't read music.

Paul McCartney, pictured in 2004

He wrote his first song at the age of 14 and shot to fame in the 1960s as a member of world's first boy band, The Beatles. The music he wrote with fellow band member John Lennon is still played today.

After The Beatles broke up in 1969 he went on to find more success with his band Wings, and is still playing to packed concert halls as a solo musician.

Paul McCartney was born on 18 June 1942, in Walton Hospital, Liverpool, where his mother had been a nurse. His father was a dance-band leader and taught Paul to play the trumpet. But when Paul was 15, there was a new style of music called Skiffle and he liked it so much he took his trumpet to a music shop and swapped it for a £15 guitar – which he still has.

DID YOU KNOW?

The rights to some of his songs are owned by singer Michael Jackson, and Paul has to pay a fee when he wants to sing them in public.

Paul and John Lennon formed The Beatles in 1959 and by 1964, with George Harrison and Ringo Starr, they were a worldwide hit. Paul said in an interview: 'John and I wrote before there were cassette players. Can you believe it was that long ago? We would often forget the songs the next day.' Everywhere they went, they were met by screaming fans. Newspaper reporters called it Beatlemania, and the world had never seen anything like it before.

Thousands of fans greeted The Beatles at Heathrow Airport, 1966

The Beatles split up in 1969, and after a couple of solo albums, Paul formed the band Wings with his wife Linda. She was a photographer, and protested she couldn't play anything, but Paul insisted that 'anyone could do it', and she learned keyboards. This meant that the couple could stay together, even when the band was on tour. Wings produced two famous songs, *Live and Let Die*, for a James Bond film, and *Mull of Kintyre*, one of the best-selling British singles ever.

Paul and Linda McCartney performing in Wings, 1976

Paul on his career: 'We thought we might have about five or ten years tops with The Beatles, but it just continued. When the ten years was up we thought, "Well now it's time to retire, isn't it?" But it wasn't, y'know, because we were still doing stuff, then I went on with Wings and that ended up a big success. I think the truth is I just always enjoy it; and if you really enjoy what you do, you don't want to stop. So people say, "Are you going to retire?" and I say, "Well you know, even if I retire I won't stop singing. I just love it too much. I won't stop writing songs." '

In 1980 John Lennon was murdered in New York, and Paul was devastated by the news. So were millions of fans, who realised that their dream of a Beatles reunion would never now come true.

Paul, who was knighted in 1997, went on to sing with Stevie Wonder and Michael Jackson, and to help with many charity concerts, including Band Aid in 1985, Ferry Aid in aid of the victims of the Zeebrugge disaster in 1987, the concert for New York after the terrorist attack on 11 September 2001, and Live 8 in 2005.

Paul McCartney plays the guitar left-handed.

DID YOU KNOW?

Paul has been made an honorary detective with the New York Police Department.

Sir Paul, who has also written classical music – the *Liverpool Oratorio* in 1991, and *Standing Stone* and *Working Classical* in the late 1990s – commented: 'I just feel amazingly lucky to be part of all these different phases and still be loving it.'

FACT FILE

- Paul is listed several times in the *Guinness Book of Records*.
- His song '*Yesterday*' has been recorded by more people than any other – there are more than 3,000 versions.
- He has sold 100 million singles, and has had 60 gold discs.
- He was given a unique rhodium disc, by Guinness, to mark this.
- He had the largest stadium audience in history, when 184,000 people paid to see him at the Maracana Stadium in Rio de Janeiro in 1990.
- He is responsible for the fastest ticket sales ever, when 20,000 tickets for two concerts in Sydney, Australia, sold in eight minutes.
- His performance of *Sgt Pepper's Lonely Hearts Club Band* with rock band U2 at Live 8 was the fastest released single in history, going on sale 45 minutes after the concert.

Paul McCartney is famous for supporting animal rights. In the 1970s he and his wife Linda became outspoken vegetarians and anti animal-testing, and Linda brought out her own brand of vegetarian food in the 1990s.

When Linda died of cancer in 1998, he kept her company going, and pledged to keep it free of genetically modified ingredients.

In 2002 he married Heather Mills, a former model and anti-land mines campaigner. They separated in 2006. Together they visited Canada to protest about seal hunting.

McCartney once said: 'If slaughterhouses had glass walls, everyone would be a vegetarian.'

Paul on seal hunting: 'People have been trying to discuss this particular seal hunt for many, many years and the answer has just been that it's happened for 500 years, it's tradition, and therefore it should continue. But we're hoping now that by bringing this amount of attention to what is actually an international problem, we will actually be able to put an end to this brutal practice.'

DID YOU KNOW?
Paul McCartney is the richest rock star in the world with an estimated fortune of £1 billion.

Paul McCartney congratulates a graduate of The Liverpool Institute for the Performing Arts.

Sir Paul has also helped fund the Liverpool Institute for the Performing Arts, which was officially opened by the Queen in 1996. It is in the same building that used to house Sir Paul's old school. In the 1980s he discovered that it was derelict, and he has paid for it to be renovated.

Evelyn Glennie

Evelyn Glennie is a world-famous percussionist – despite the fact that she became deaf when she was 12. She travels the world playing drums, cymbals, and even pieces of scaffolding.

Evelyn Glennie in action.

FACT FILE

Evelyn's firsts:

Her first recording, in 1989, won a Grammy award.

She is the first and only full-time professional classical percussion soloist.

She gave the first ever percussion recital and percussion concerto in the history of the Royal Academy of Music (which was founded in 1822).

DID YOU KNOW:
Evelyn loves to travel on motorbikes, and got her full motorbike licence in 2001.

She has said: 'The thing about playing percussion is that you can create all these emotions that can be sometimes beautiful, sometimes really ugly, or sometimes sweet, sometimes as big as King Kong and so on. And so there can be a real riot out there, or it can be so refined.'

'Anything you strike, anything you shake or rattle, or just anything that can be picked up, you can create a sound.'

Evelyn was born in Aberdeenshire, Scotland in 1965. She grew up on a farm, and played harmonica and clarinet as a child. When she was eight she began to lose her hearing, but she began to play the snare drum, and decided she wanted to do it for a living. She decided on her career when she was 15. She studied piano and percussion at the Royal College of Music in London, where she found out that there had never been anyone else who made a living as a solo percussionist. But she wasn't going to change her mind!

Evelyn playing vibraphone with a string ensemble.

Evelyn wants audiences to think about her music, rather than her deafness. She can hear sounds and distinguish them, though she cannot hear them the way she could as a child. She can't make out clearly what people are saying, so she reads lips. When she performs, she performs barefoot, and 'hears' her own instrument and the orchestra by feeling vibrations through the floor and in her own body.

She says: 'Before my teen years, I was losing my hearing pretty quickly, and I was getting very, very angry. I was beginning to become an angry person because of that.

'And my teacher, you know, he said, "Evelyn just put your hand on the ball of the tympani, on the copper ball," and this I did and, you know, I felt something,

and so we would go on like that. And then suddenly my hands would be placed on the thin walls of the room, and he would tune the two drums to a very wide interval. [An interval is the space between two notes.]

'And so he would say, "Which drum am I playing?" And I might say, "Oh, the lower drum." "And how do you know that?" I said, "Well, I can feel it from here to here." And so he would play the other drum. I said, "Yes, I can tell the difference." I suppose I don't hear things, but I listen, if you know what I mean. And there is a big difference between hearing and listening. So it's like a conversation, you know. When you speak to someone, it's one on one, and that's exactly how I play.'

Evelyn is the patron of many charities supporting young musicians, and people with a variety of disabilities.

Evelyn Glennie feels the vibrations as she plays.

After winning the Grammy award in 1989, Evelyn has gone on to make many more recordings and videos and has written an autobiography called *Good Vibrations*. She has composed music for TV dramas and adverts, worked with many performers and composers, including Björk and DJ MJ Cole, and has commissioned more than 120 percussion works from a wide range of composers. Jazz composer Django Bates wrote a piece for her called *My Dream Kitchen*, in which all the instruments are kitchen utensils.

Evelyn performs with a variety of orchestras and musicians. She gives around 110 concerts per year, and spends up to four months a year touring in the USA alone, as well as giving master classes and performing in schools. Some of her shows are totally improvised.

Evelyn with her exhaust pipe simtak.

In any one performance, she can be playing up to 60 different instruments which may include flower pots, kitchen utensils and other ordinary objects. Evelyn owns nearly 1,400 percussion instruments, including those of her own design: the cymbal tree, pieces of scaffolding, and the simtak, which is an exhaust pipe played with triangle beaters.

One critic said this to describe Evelyn's performance: 'This thrilling, hyperkinetic, wild woman bangs, caresses, shakes, strokes, strikes, scrapes, and generally beats the tar out of a huge array of all kinds of percussion instruments; congas, vibes, cowbells, cymbals, marimba, her own instrument creations, up to about 60 instruments in any given show (she travels with up to two TONS of gear). By playing barefoot, Evelyn is able to experience the music fully.'

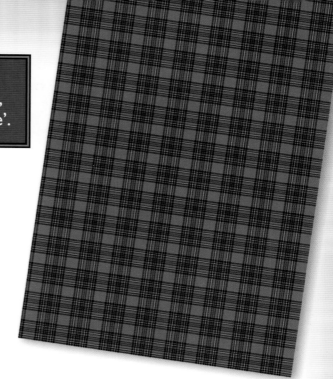

Evelyn plays all the conventional percussion instruments (including xylophone, marimba, vibraphone, drum kit, blocks, chimes, bells, tambourines, tam tams and gongs) and has been described as a wizard on a wide variety of ethnic instruments (such as congas, bongos, log drums, gamelan, wind gongs, rain trees, maracas and guiros).

She designs and sells her own percussion instruments and accessories, including a new type of cymbal called 'Glennie's Garbage', made from sheet metal. She has called the sound 'really trashy'.

Evelyn has also used pieces of scaffolding to make instruments. She is always looking for interesting materials to play with. She also plays the Great Highland bagpipes. But she says: 'If I truly had to be stranded on a desert island, then I think the snare drum would be my instrument.'

PERSONAL FACT FILE

Full name: **Evelyn Elizabeth Ann Glennie**

Birthplace: **North of Aberdeen, Scotland**

Star sign: **Cancer**

Favourite colours: **Red and purple**

Favourite food: **Anything Italian, plus shortbread, Earl Grey tea and chocolate.**

Favourite musicians: **Maxim Vengerov (violinist), Terry Bozzio (percussionist), The Chieftains (a traditional Irish music group), Bela Fleck (banjo player)**

Never travels without: **Her Gameboy**

Evelyn Glennie amidst an array of percussion instruments.

Global Warming

Elm stays cool

American interests must come first in beating global warming.

Elm: 'Doing what's best for my people'

This is US President Bernard Elm's tough message at a world leaders' meeting on reducing any harmful effects of gas and petrol.

Out of step with many scientists who say this is a main cause of air pollution, he told reporters:

'I am going to do what's best for my people.'

The president will offer ideas for safer energy. He stubbornly backed those who say that rising world temperatures and ice melting at the North and South Poles are due mainly to nature.

Heated debate on global warming

Political correspondent **Maria Lee**

British officials believe US President Bernard Elm, seeking to improve his world image, will offer new ideas at next week's London summit for reducing global warming.

But he will turn down any measures that could harm American interests.

He stressed to reporters that he would protect Americans from costly measures in reducing the use of non-renewable fuels like oil and gas.

The USA is among the biggest users and producers of these fuels. It has refused to support the 1997 Kyoto decision by most nations to set targets to reduce their use. The USA did not accept they were the main reason for harmful greenhouse gases that cause global warming.

Elm feels the heat in Texas, yesterday

Many scientists believe there is enough evidence proving that fossil fuels are a major cause of damaging climate changes. Their use raises temperatures, and speeds up melting of ice at the Poles, causing world-wide floods.

The ✦ Herald
Founded 1921   Issue 26,527

Editorial

World leaders must not risk our future by ignoring those like Britain's chief scientist Sir David King. He is calling for urgent steps to reduce use of those fuels that create harmful gases and upset the weather.

Some scientists agree the climate is warming up enough to speed the melting of ice at the Poles, causing the sea to flood low-lying farming areas and submerge small islands. However, they insist this is just part of a natural, historical cycle that will reverse.

Professor King and many other scientists disagree. They believe ever-increasing use of fossil fuel like petrol produces too much harmful carbon dioxide that is the real cause of the global warming that threatens to kill wildlife and swamp much of Britain.

King says a three-degree rise in temperature over the next 100 years could produce inland deserts as well as rising sea water, leading to world hunger. Use of safer fuels like solar or wind power might slow this down.

A new survey by the Botanical Society of the British Isles claims mean temperatures in Central England have already gone up by one degree in the past 20 years.

Even if Professor King is wrong, world leaders must not take chances with the lives of future generations. We must stop arguing, move to safer fuels and cut use of fossil fuels now.

The Herald

Netherby run rings round Moreton

Netherby Rovers booked a place in their first ever Conference Football League Final, beating Moreton 2–1 before a largely home crowd of 10,000. This gives them a 3–1 aggregate with their away single-goal win from last week's away semi-final.

Moreton scared them briefly in the first half when Nathan Haram slipped in from the right wing to snatch a loose ball and punch it past surprised Rovers' goal-keeper, Pete Smith, only ten minutes into the game.

Rovers struggled to get an equaliser, but goalie Smith was hardly troubled again. Moreton spent most of the first half on the defensive, trying to take back possession, but were rarely out of their own half. The homeside's persistent attacking paid off five minutes from

Moreton fans brave it at the Netherby Ground

the interval. Full-back Shanta Phipps trapped a long but wayward pass meant for Moreton's Haram. He powered it down the left side to half-back John Howard. He dribbled past two opponents and skied it to the centre. Striker Bill Stead picked it up neatly and left-footed into the corner of the Moreton net.

Moreton seemed to give up, especially after Rovers were awarded a penalty over a trip twenty minutes into the second half. Stead fooled Moreton goalie Joe Hinton and hooked a hard one into the right corner as he dived left.

Moreton rallied for about five minutes with swift cross-field passing attacks in the Netherby half. But the defence held. Victorious Rovers were back on attack when the final whistle went amid roars from the home crowd.

Early inspiration from Haram, but it wasn't to be enough

Rovers roar to their first-ever final

Rampaging Netherby Rovers charged their way to a first-ever Conference League final last night. They crushed rivals Moreton 2–1 to the shrieking delight of the largely home, scarf-waving crowd.

Rovers ground down the visitors for a total 3–1 victory after winning away last week by a single goal in the first round of the semi-final.

Scrappy Moreton were really only in the game for the first ten minutes. A surprise first goal from slippery Natham Haram on the right wing only served to rally Rovers. Netherby goalkeeper Pete Smith was hardly ever troubled again.

The visitors spent most of the first half just trying to deny possession to the homeside. But the Rovers pinned Moreton firmly in their own territory. Rovers' hard running, quick passing and persistence paid off when they snatched the ball five minutes from the interval.

Netherby full-back Shanta Phipps neatly trapped a wildly loose pass meant for Moreton's Haram on one of his few forays into the Rover's half. Brown skied it hard and long to the alert half, Ron Howard. He cunningly dribbled past two players and centred to fleet-footed striker Bill Stead. A well-aimed flick from his left foot pounded into the corner of Moreton's net, leaving the goal-keeper stranded on the wrong side.

By now, Moreton were looking tired. They struggled through the second half to hold back a constant tide of attacks. They seemed to give up after conceding

Decisive play from Stead takes Rovers to the final

Jubilation on the terraces

a penalty for a clearly deliberate trip twenty minutes into the second half. Wily Stead fooled Moreton goalie Joe Hinton to go left, then rammed the ball into the right-hand corner.

Rovers were about to swamp them again when the final whistle went to wild jubilation from the home crowd.

Plants on the move

Some plants have travelled great distances from their native lands. Some moved accidentally as seeds caught on clothing, vehicles or goods. Others were transported intentionally to be grown elsewhere. Did these new introductions have positive or negative results?

The potato

The potato originated in the Andes mountains of South America. The plant was taken to Europe in the 16th century by explorers such as Sir Francis Drake. At first, it was believed to be poisonous, but in time, it was widely adopted as a cheap, nutritious food. Settlers took the potato to North America and today it is grown in cool, wet places all over the world.

- *About 200 different wild species of potato grow in the Andes.*
- *The name 'potato' comes from 'batata', the Spanish word for 'sweet potato'.*
- *The potato is the fifth highest production crop in the world.*
- *Potatoes that have gone green can be poisonous.*

potato plants

Sugar cane

Sugar cane probably originated in India. As people travelled and traded, the plant was transported westwards towards the Middle East and Europe. At first, sugar was a rare commodity but when Europeans took it to South America and the Caribbean, large plantations, worked by slaves, began producing it in huge amounts. This led to sweets, syrups and chocolate – and worldwide tooth decay.

- *Sugar cane is a type of tropical grass.*
- *The sugar is extracted by evaporating water from the sap.*
- *Sugar cane is one of the raw materials used to make biodiesel fuels.*

sugar cane

Tobacco

The tobacco plant is native to the tropical regions of South and Central America. The early explorers brought it back to Europe, where it was first thought to be a wonder drug that would cure all kinds of disease. Little did they know that smoking tobacco would become a major *cause* of disease and death.

Sir Walter Raleigh transported it to North America where it was grown in huge plantations, using the labour of African slaves. The tobacco leaves were dried in barns before being exported to Europe where smoking was all the rage.

Tobacco, in the form of cigarettes, has now spread all over the world – along with smoking-related diseases, such as cancer, bronchitis and heart disease.

- *In South America, tobacco was originally smoked by priests known as shamans.*

- *Tobacco was not always smoked: native Americans chewed the leaves, while in Europe, finely-powdered 'snuff' was sniffed into the nose.*

tobacco leaves

The early travels of the potato, sugar-cane and tobacco.

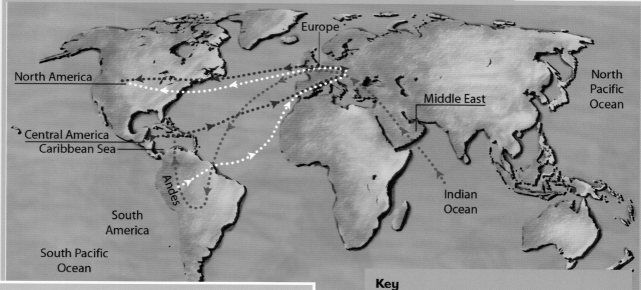

Europe

North America

Middle East

North Pacific Ocean

Central America
Caribbean Sea

Andes

Indian Ocean

South America

South Pacific Ocean

The world's top growers
(in million metric tons)

	Potato	Sugar cane	Tobacco
China	75	390	2.4
Russia	37	282	0.9
India	25	90	0.6

Key

POTATO ‒ ‒ ‒ ‒ ‒ ‒ ‒ ‒
Distance travelled: Approximately 15,500 km

SUGAR CANE ‒ ‒ ‒ ‒ ‒ ‒ ‒
Distance travelled: Approximately 18,625 km

TOBACCO ‒ ‒ ‒ ‒ ‒ ‒ ‒
Distance travelled: Approximately 14,530 km

The World's Favourite Fruit

Almost everyone loves bananas; they are the world's most popular fruit. The plant, which originated in southeast Asia, proved easy to cultivate and transport. A tasty and important crop, today is grown in many countries, and is eaten in even more!

The history of the banana

The banana originated in south-east Asia, in the area around Malaysia. The sweet, creamy fruit was so popular that the plant was taken by migrants and traders to India and China. It travelled to Madagascar with Islamic traders, from where it was taken to West Africa – along with ivory and African slaves. Portuguese sailors, exploring the region, transported the banana back to Europe, and to the Canary Islands, where plantations began to supply popular demand. From there, the plant was taken to the 'New World' – to Central America and the Caribbean, where bananas are still grown today.

flower   hands of fruit   stem

The fruits point upwards as they grow above the flower.

Banana cultivation

The banana plant requires hot, humid conditions and a well-drained soil. The plant shoots from a bulb-like rootstock, known as a rhizome, producing a stalk that grows up to nine metres tall. Flower buds grow from the stalk, opening into rows of tiny flowers, which gradually develop into 'hands' of bananas containing 15–30 fruits (or 'fingers' as they are known). When the plants are about nine months old, the large hands are harvested green and immediately start to ripen. Within 36 hours, they are loaded on to ships and, two weeks later – yellow, sweet and ripe – are sold in shops around the world.

The banana trade

Bananas are important in international trade and are worth £5 billion per year. The fruit is grown in about 130 countries but even some of the largest producers, such as India, Brazil and China, produce it as a staple food rather than for the export market. The major exporters are mainly in South and Central America, and include Ecuador, Costa Rica and Colombia. For these countries, bananas are an important source of employment and provide a vital income from richer, developed countries, which are the major importers. Trade with Britain alone is worth £750 million.

The average banana plant grows to 9 m in height

Distribution of world banana production (2000–2004)

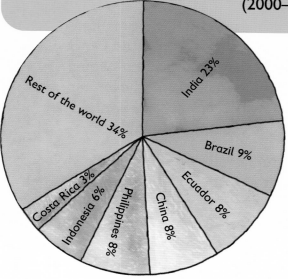

India 23%
Brazil 9%
Ecuador 8%
China 8%
Philippines 8%
Indonesia 6%
Costa Rica 3%
Rest of the world 34%

BANANA FACTS

- Alexander the Great tasted the banana on a military campaign in India in about 327 BC.
- A banana plant is not a tree because it does not have a woody stem. It is the world's largest herb.
- The word 'banana' comes from the Arabic word 'banan', meaning 'finger'.

Distribution of world banana imports (1999–2003)

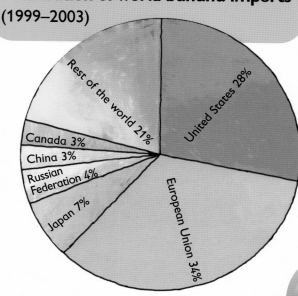

United States 28%
European Union 34%
Japan 7%
Russian Federation 4%
China 3%
Canada 3%
Rest of the world 21%

Do Games Rot the Brain?

Welcome once again to 'Have Your Say' – the programme that seeks out the truth!

This week we are looking at video games – so expect some strong reactions! Some people think these games encourage violent behaviour, whilst others believe that they're educational and fun.

So what's the truth? Are video games bad for you? Listen to what Harry has to say!

Video games are a complete waste of time and children should be banned from playing them. After all, you wouldn't give your children cigarettes to smoke, would you?

Scientific studies prove that computer games are addictive, just like cigarettes. I know kids who spend hours playing video games – they're obsessed! They don't have any other interests and they never read books. They can't concentrate long enough!

Scientific studies also link gaming to violent behaviour. It's hardly surprising that kids get wound up when they're playing. In a video game, the more violent you are, the more points you score – so violence is rewarded!

Gaming also results in poor social skills. Video games stunt the parts of the brain that deal with controlling behaviour and getting on with others. One researcher stated that children need to 'play outside with other children and interact and communicate with others as much as possible.' Obviously, you can't do that cooped up indoors, on your own, in front of a computer game, can you?

Even if you could, that sort of lifestyle is unhealthy. Children who play computer games get unfit, suffer eye strain and may have fits. Many gamers get 'Nintendo Grip', and can't hold a pencil properly.

Some people think that banning things is a bad idea. Well, I've got news for them! My friend was banned from his PlayStation for a week, and guess what? He started playing chess with his sister!

Well, it's clear what Harry's view is on the subject! Let's hear what our reporter, Miles Perry, has found out.

Yes, Claire, computer games certainly get a bad press in some quarters. But they have their champions, too.

As we heard from Harry, games may be addictive. Some studies show that seriously addicted gamers neglect school work, family, friends and their own health. However, many people think the term 'addiction' is unfair. For example, someone engrossed in a book would not be accused of 'addiction'. Gamers argue that non-gamers don't realise how absorbing games can be.

There are also two sides to the argument about games and violence. On the one hand, there are studies suggesting a direct link between aggression and game playing. On the other hand, there are studies suggesting that games don't make children violent. In fact, it may be good for children to play out their aggressive feelings on screen!

So how true is this image of social outcasts who spend all their time in their rooms? Certainly, gaming can be lonely – it's just you and your computer! Nevertheless, gamers often belong to strong communities, online and in the playground. They swap tips and strategies and compare experiences. All this helps to strengthen their social skills, not erode them.

On balance, most experts agree that parental guidance is important. Computer games can bring strong benefits, for example good coordination and problem-solving skills – and they're great fun! But, like most of the nice things in life, a little goes a long way. One researcher summed it up when she advised parents to aim for a balance in their child's life. Sports are important, reading's important. Just think of computer games as one more component in a child's exploration of what's out there in society.

SURFING WARS!

Should kids use the Internet? Some people think that the Internet is dangerous and makes kids lazy. Others believe that the Internet has opened up a whole new world for children. What do you think? Read this article by 10-year-old Kerry Mason, and post your views!

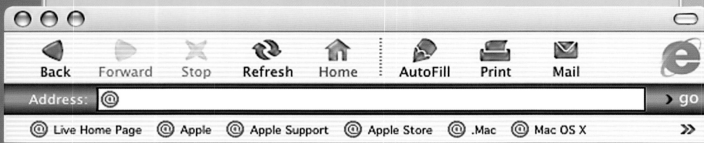

| Back | Forward | Stop | Refresh | Home | AutoFill | Print | Mail |

Address: @   > go

@ Live Home Page   @ Apple   @ Apple Support   @ Apple Store   @ .Mac   @ Mac OS X   »

Favorites   History   Search   Scrapbook   Page Holder

The Internet is a brilliant way to learn, have fun and keep up with friends. If used properly, it's a great tool.

I've never seen any upsetting images online. My computer has good parental controls, so these images are blocked. On the other hand, I *have* seen violent images on television – there's no way to block that! In any case, it's a violent world – surely it's better for us to see what's out there and learn how to deal with it?

My parents trust me because they've explained the risks and laid down a few simple rules – like never giving my address online. If there are dangerous strangers out there, I've never met them. I love my BMX online chatroom: it's a great way to keep up with the sport.

The Internet is also ideal for homework. Some kids lose track of time, or get distracted by games online, but that's their fault – not the Internet's! I always set a time limit and keep on task. Then I reward myself with an online game or chat when I've finished!

Books are OK but the information is often out of date and usually from one viewpoint. On the Internet, you can access up-to-date information from lots of different points of view. It's easy to check information by cross-checking on other sites, to make sure they agree.

People complain about bad spelling and grammar on the Internet – but at least the Internet gets kids writing! In any case, it's unfair to compare online writing to formal writing. It's like comparing a chat with friends to an assembly presentation!

My mum says, 'A bad workman always blames his tools.' I think she's right – the Internet is only as good as the person using it!

Comments

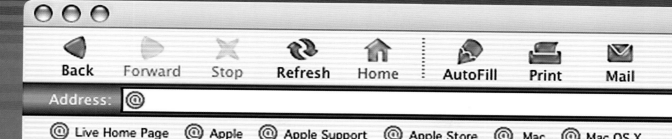

It's sick and violent!

The Internet is full of sick and violent images. At best, this material is upsetting. At worst, children soak up this rubbish. The result? Violent teenagers and rising street crime. What is the attraction?

Posted at 6.19 pm by Foxy

Re: It's sick and violent!

That's so reactionary! As Kerry pointed out, that's what parental controls are there for – they screen this stuff out. You can't protect your kids. The best thing is to be open with them – talk about what they see, and trust them!

Posted at 6.30 pm by Cooldude

Re: It's sick and violent!

I'm with Foxy – the controls don't work! Recently, so-called 'friends' from an online chatroom dared my granddaughter to do dangerous things. My son blocked this site, but there are hundreds more like it on the Internet. Children are too inexperienced to be trusted. How can we be sure our kids are safe?

Posted at 7.00 pm by Northerner

What about homework?

Your kids *aren't* safe! They face dangers all the time – like crossing the road! The Internet is great, all that information at the click of a mouse. Homework has never been so much fun.

Posted at 7.10 pm by Cooldude

Re: What about homework?

I have to disagree with this! The Internet is not a good way to research information. My son uses it for homework and it takes hours! First, he's distracted by online games. Second, there are only a few sites with good information and they're difficult to find. Third, when he does find the information he wants, he can't trust it. Web content is not checked like books are. Often, his hard-won facts are wrong! And the standard of spelling and grammar online is appalling!

Posted at 7.20 pm by Foxy

The voice of reason

Hey guys, calm down! You're just proving Kerry's point: the Internet is only as good as the person using it. You're scared because you don't think your kids will cope with what's out there. But denying them access to the Internet won't make the bad stuff go away! This is the world they're living in. It's better to prepare them for it – trust them, and keep talking!

Posted at 7.30 by Cooldude

Library Questionnaire

Share your views!

We want to know what you thought of the last book you borrowed from the library.

Book title ....

Author ....

1. How much did you enjoy it?

    ☐ A lot   ☐ A bit   ☐ Not at all

2. How many stars would you give it?

    ....

3. What was the best thing about it?

    ....

4. What was the worst thing about it?

    ....

5. Who do you think would like this book?

    ....

6. What sort of books do you like to read?
   Circle as many words as you like.

Stories	Magical	Adventure
Real life	Sports	Facts
Romance	Funny	Internet
Animals	Mystery	History
Audio books	Homework	Music

I had a *book* on wild animals last week. The pictures were great, but there wasn't much information. It was too young for me. I don't know what to put for questions 1 and 2.

I like *books* with facts about animals and funny history *books*. But if I say 'animals', 'facts', 'history' and 'funny', they might think I mean funny animal stories, and facts about history. Boring!

What's on the Menu?

The text below is taken from official government guidelines for school meals.

Guidance for school caterers on implementing national nutritional standards

This chapter summarises compulsory nutritional standards, which are set out in legislation. These are **minimum standards**. If your Local Education Authority or school has set higher nutritional standards, you should meet those.

The standards say that lunches for primary school pupils must contain at least one item from each of the following food groups.

- **starchy foods** such as bread, potatoes, rice and pasta. Starchy food cooked in oil or fat should not be served more than **three** times a week.

- **fruit and a vegetable** must be available **every day**. Fruit based desserts must be available **twice** a week.

- **milk** and **dairy** foods.

- **meat**, **fish** and alternative sources of **protein**. Red meat must be served at least **twice a week**. Fish must be served at least **once a week**.

This questionaire is aimed at the people who prepare school meals. How easy is it to fill in the following questionnaire? How useful will the information be, and how well does it link up with the guidelines?

Fill in the questionnaire and return to the _____ in the envelope provided by 29th July.

How much time to you spend preparing the daily meal?	*Circle one* 1 hour or less 1-2 hours 2-3 hours
How often do the children choose the vegetarian option?	*Circle one* usually sometimes seldom
Do you provide alternative sources of protein daily?	Yes/No
How many times per week do you serve starchy food cooked in oil or fat?	*Circle one* less than twice a week twice a week 3-4 times a week
Do the majority of children usually choose the fresh fruit or the fruit dessert?	*Circle one* fresh fruit fruit dessert

How are Mountains Formed?

Have you heard the expression 'as old as the hills'? It suggests that mountains are very old indeed. In fact, considering the age of the Earth (4,600 million years), many of the highest mountains are actually quite young. For example, the Himalayas were formed only 50 million years ago. Dinosaurs were already extinct!

The Himalayas

Different mountains are formed in different ways.

The crust does not go round the Earth like a skin. It is made of large pieces which fit together a bit like a jigsaw. These are called *plates* and they move slowly on the soft rock underneath. Some carry continents (continental plates) and others carry oceans (oceanic plates). Over millions of years, the plates move to new positions. This means that the shape of the earth is always changing.

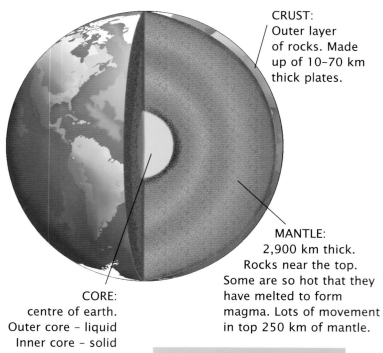

CRUST:
Outer layer of rocks. Made up of 10–70 km thick plates.

MANTLE:
2,900 km thick. Rocks near the top. Some are so hot that they have melted to form magma. Lots of movement in top 250 km of mantle.

CORE:
centre of earth.
Outer core – liquid
Inner core – solid

The structure of the Earth

Fold mountains

Fold mountains are formed when two plates (two continental or one continental and one oceanic) crash together. As one plate gradually slides under the other, particles of rock (called sediment) build up. This eventually turns to solid rock (sedimentary rock) because of heat and pressure. Over time, the movement of the two plates forces the rock upwards. Nearer the surface, huge forces squeeze the rock and it buckles upwards in a series of folds.

India used to be a long way from the rest of Asia. Long ago, the plate carrying India moved closer to Asia and the collision created the Himalayan mountain range. People have found rocks containing the fossils of sea animals high up in the mountains and this shows that the rock was once on the seabed as part of the oceanic plate.

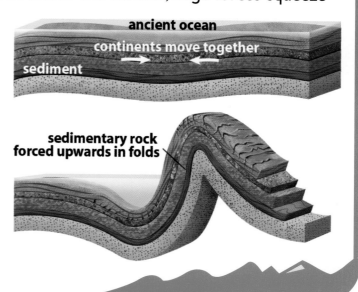

Block mountains and rift valleys

The earth's crust has many cracks which are called *faults*. These faults can go down many kilometres. If two faults are close together, the chunk of crust can be pushed up or down because of the huge pressure. When the rock is pushed up in this way, *block mountains* are formed. The Sierra Nevada range in California was made like that. If the rock is pushed down, then a *rift valley* is formed. The most famous one is the Great Rift Valley in East Africa. It is nearly 5,000 km long and 160 km wide in places.

The Great Rift Valley

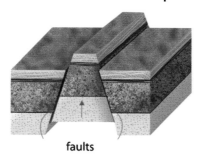

faults

Block mountain

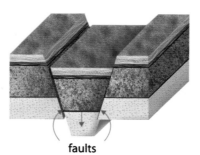

faults

Rift valley

Mountains and Global Warming

Many scientists believe that the world's temperature will rise 1.5°C in the next 50 years. This is a huge increase in a short time and it is known as global warming. Why is it happening?

Modern-day living produces many so-called 'greenhouse gases'. Burning fossil fuels such as coal, oil and gas produces carbon dioxide and car exhausts emit nitrogen oxides. These gases form a blanket which allow the rays of the sun to pass through, but prevent heat from bouncing back into space. This creates a 'greenhouse effect' resulting in climate changes such as global warming.

layer of greenhouse gases – some of which are needed to stop the Earth getting too cold

rays of sun

Some heat is bounced back onto earth.

How is the mountain environment affected?

The temperature falls by about 0.6°C every 100 metres of altitude. This results in different ecosystems at different heights above sea level. Global warming affects the mountain ecosystems. As the air temperature rises, animals and plants in lower level habitats move up the mountains to find the cooler environments that suit them. Records over the last 100 years show that trees in the Alps are working their way up the mountains at a rate of about 4 metres every 10 years. In some areas, the change is even faster. This habitat change means that organisms which live highest up the mountains are the hardest hit because they have nowhere to go. The mountain top is effectively an island – and they cannot get off. Animal and plant species are declining as a result of the changes in temperature.

The Alpine environment is changing quickly.

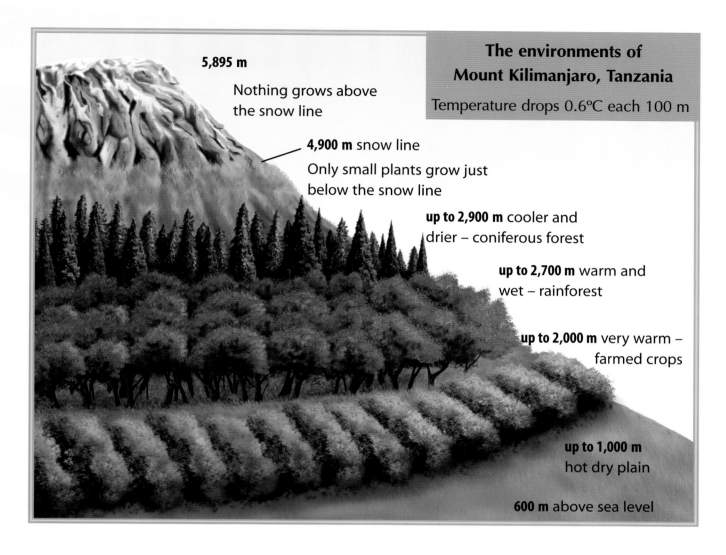

The environments of Mount Kilimanjaro, Tanzania

Temperature drops 0.6°C each 100 m

5,895 m

Nothing grows above the snow line

4,900 m snow line

Only small plants grow just below the snow line

up to 2,900 m cooler and drier – coniferous forest

up to 2,700 m warm and wet – rainforest

up to 2,000 m very warm – farmed crops

up to 1,000 m hot dry plain

600 m above sea level

Other effects of global warming

- Quickly melting glaciers increase the risk of flooding.
- Glaciers are melting earlier in spring, so all the fresh water from the mountains has dried up by the summer.
- Less water will be available from the mountains because the glaciers are melting away.
- As a result of drought, soil and vegetation will be drier, increasing risk of fire.
- Rising water temperatures create unsuitable conditions for river wildlife so their numbers are declining. The creatures that feed on them will also decline as their food suppy becomes more limited.

A glacier melting

Mountain regions all over the world have had their own unique climates and ecosystems for millions of years. Rapid climate change, caused by global warming, may be transforming them forever.

Mini-monsters

The world we live in is full of millions of micro-organisms. These include microbes (bacteria, viruses and fungi) and insects that are so tiny they can only be seen under a microscope. However, they can cause a great deal of trouble – to people and their homes.

Your body – under attack!

Bacteria are the oldest living things and many can live inside the human body. They reproduce and can cause disease by attacking the cells. Usually people can get rid of these germs quickly because the body fights back. Sometimes, however, there are so many and they are so strong that they cause illnesses such as sore throats and stomach upsets.

There are also even more powerful microbes, called viruses, at work in the human body. They were not discovered until long after bacteria because they are far too small to be seen under an ordinary microscope. Viruses cannot exist on their own. They have to invade healthy body cells to survive.

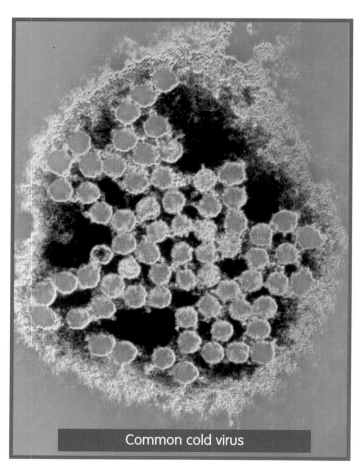
Common cold virus

How does a virus work?

Every cell in the human body contains a nucleus. This is a sort of command centre – it tells the cell what to do. The virus enters the nucleus and takes over. It then orders the cell to make lots of new viruses. While this is happening, the body does not know the virus is there. At last they burst out of the cell. This means that poisons are let out and this is what makes someone feel achy when they have a cold or flu.

Bacteria and viruses are on the loose...

- on shared toothbrushes or glasses.

- in water droplets in coughs and sneezes – viruses can travel up to 2 m. (Coughs and sneezes really do spread diseases!).

- in plaque on teeth. Bacteria + sugar in food → acid → attack the enamel on tooth

- in saliva from dogs and cats.

- from abroad! Foreign microbes upset the ones that live harmlessly in the body all the time. This makes people ill.

- in food that is not prepared or cooked properly.

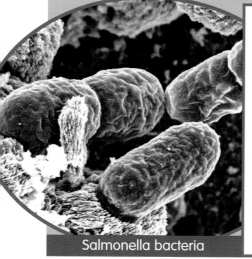
Salmonella bacteria

Hygiene Rules OK!

- Wash hands before touching food.
- Cover food to prevent bacteria carried by flies.
- Use different knives for raw and cooked meat.
- Clean work surfaces carefully.

- Cook food through fully to kill bugs such as salmonella.
- Keep raw and cooked food in different parts of the fridge so they cannot touch each other.

Microscopic life in the house

There could be 10 million microscopic dust mites in your bed tonight, feasting on tiny pieces of skin! They are harmless in themselves, but some people are allergic to their droppings, which can cause itchy eyes, wheezing and sneezing.

Fungi are moulds which live on damp surfaces and cause black stains and slimy patches on walls. Their spores make some people wheeze. (Dry and wet rot are other kinds of fungi which attack wood and paintwork in the house.)

Stay alert! Be on the lookout for bad microbes!

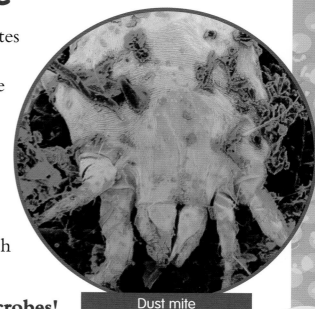
Dust mite

Marvellous Microbes

When people think of bacteria, viruses and fungi, they usually think of germs. However, there are many useful microbes that work away to help us.

Good microbes in the body

The human body contains millions of bacteria. Of these, 95% are harmless, and many do important jobs. For example, some help protect against harmful microbes; others live in the digestive system and help digest food. In addition, some people like to eat 'live' yoghurt which contains huge numbers of bacteria to add to those already in the gut.

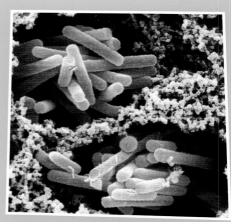

Yoghurt bacteria

Using the bad guys

Smallpox was a killer disease caused by a virus. Edward Jenner, an 18th-century country doctor, was fascinated by the old wives' tale that milkmaids could not catch smallpox. He believed the milkmaids became immune because of a related non-fatal cattle disease, cowpox. He noticed that milkmaids who caught cowpox developed blisters full of pus on their hands, and thought this was important. Therefore in 1798, he introduced the pus into cuts on a boy's arm to give him cowpox. Jenner then deliberately gave him smallpox in order to test his theory. The boy became a little unwell but soon recovered.

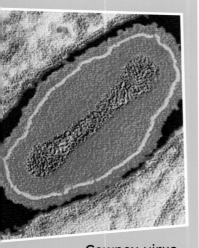

Cowpox virus

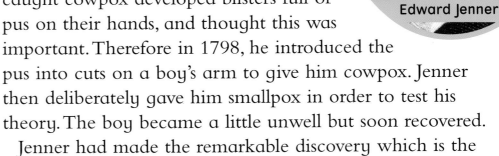

Edward Jenner

Jenner had made the remarkable discovery which is the basis of vaccination today: that a weak version of a disease stimulates the body to make antibodies to fight the infection and protect itself. However, Jenner still did not understand what caused the disease in the first place. It was not until 1885 that Louis Pasteur proved that microbes caused infection and started to develop vaccines to provide protection.

The word 'vaccination' comes from the Latin word 'vacca' meaning 'cow'.